Long Dista

Walks

Volume Two
The Yorkshire Dales

You don't need to have an official route to get you out into the open air. You don't have to wait for the Countryside Commission to say "OK you can go". You don't have to follow the crowds. In this country there are thousands of long distance routes for walkers that have never suffered an official blessing (and are all the better for that) and any walker with initiative can plan his own itineraries simply by linking the public rights of way recorded on current issues of 1" Ordnance maps. There is positively no end to the routes that can be worked out. You may follow high level tracks over the hills; or circuit mountain watersheds; or march the boundary of your county or any other; or trace old drove roads; or go from point A to point B, whether A and B are called castles, Roman camps, stone circles or whatever; or visit your maiden aunt in Bognor; or cross the country on canal towpaths; or follow rivers from source to sea.

And all on foot, using rights of way, causing no trespass and needing no permission. The map of England is an oyster very rich in pearls. Plan your own marathon and do something never done before, something you will enjoy, a route that will take you to places often read about but never yet seen. You will be on your own, unhampered by human beings en bloc, relying on your own resources to complete what you set out to do. Preferably go alone and do it off your own bat, for it is the solitary walker, always, who most closely identifies himself with his surroundings, who observes as he goes along, who really feels the satisfaction of achievement. If you must have a friend choose one who is quiet.

— **from 'A Coast to Coast Walk',**
Alfred Wainwright, 1973.

Long Distance Walks

Volume Two

The Yorkshire Dales

by
Tony Wimbush
and
Alan Gott

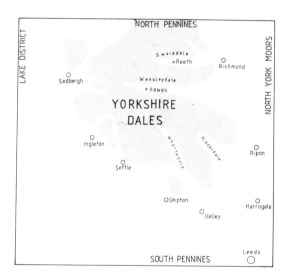

Dalesman Books
1982

The Dalesman Publishing Company Ltd.,
Clapham, via Lancaster, LA2 8EB

First published 1982

© Tony Wimbush, 1982

ISBN 0 85206 676 7

To
J. C. Wimbush
(1913-1981)

Printed in Great Britain
Alf Smith & Co., Bradford, West Yorkshire.

Contents

Cover photograph by Geoffrey N. Wright.

Title page photograph of walkers on the Ulfkil Stride by Chris Steer.

Note: The inclusion of a route in this book should not be taken as implying a legal right of way.

Acknowledgements: Many thanks go to the individuals who have contributed in the preparation of this book. These include David Joy and Dave Jeffery for advice and suggestions; Alison Metcalfe for typing; Peter Barker, Stuart Pailor, Dave Burland, A. T. Ashworth, Colin Newton, Richard French, Ken Piggin, Peter Bayes, Geoff Bell, Elizabeth Green, Ian Grant, Tony Perkins, Melvin Boldison, Tom Burns and Marie-Eugene Brown for helpful information. I wish to thank the following for the quotation of extracts: The Westmorland Gazette from *A Coast to Coast Walk* ; Country Life Limited from *Broad Acres.*

Preface

THE backcloth for the second volume on this series of guides to the long distance walks in the North of England is the Yorkshire Dales: the great northern dales of Swaledale, Wensleydale, Wharfedale, Ribblesdale, Airedale and Nidderdale. It is a country of high fells and wild moors, of green pastures and white limestone, of ruined castles and abbeys, and of noble houses and village inns. Many have attempted to capture the Dales landscape in words and pictures, but there is no substitute for the reality of this wild country. And what better way to comprehend such immense beauty than on foot striding across the landscape; to traverse the tops; to climb the dividing ridges; and to trek along the watersheds and valleys; to go on and on from dawn to dusk, or even dawn again; to know the natural world in all the changing seasons; in all its moods and rhythms; and in all its subtle interplay of light, form, colour and texture. Truly this is the way to discover and understand a country.

Interwoven with all this is the lure of a challenge – the irresistible desire to test and stretch physical and mental capabilities. No doubt this is why the Three Peaks of Yorkshire and the Pennine Way have attracted so much interest. It is hoped that the other walks in this book will be just as stimulating and introduce new horizons to the experienced long distance walker as well as the novice. Although the routes have been arranged into their recognised categories for ease of reference I would encourage the reader to adapt these to his own personal aims and ambitions. For example, the 33 mile Ulfkil Stride, an annually organised walk, can be undertaken at anytime as, say, a two-day expedition, while the 80 mile Dales Way may be comtemplated as a non-stop ultra-long distance challenge by the more ambitious. I also hope that the book will help create fresh ideas and encourage walkers to devise their own adventures for which the scope is unlimited.

Finally, a reminder of the rewards: the exaltation of a good day out on the hills when mind and body merge into an effortless rhythm with the surrounding world, and all is in tune; the panoramas of inexhaustible beauty and inspiration; the spirit of the eternal hills and the friendships that it engenders; and not least the experiences and memories that will last a lifetime.

Tony Wimbush,
December 1981.

Introductory Notes
Types of Long Distance Walking

ONLY walks of 20 miles or more have been regarded as long distance. For ease of reference these have been arranged into the following four categories, characterised as shown.

Open Challenge Walks
- Can be attempted at any time.
- Specific route and distance to be completed.
- Route description, certificates and badges are often issued by a walk secretary.
- Route usually has to be completed as a continuous exercise often within a time limit.
- Navigational ability essential.
- Essentially a challenge.

Challenge Events
- Date and start time are fixed.
- Entry by application form and fee.
- Maximum number of participants.
- Route is defined by a series of checkpoints where tallies must be punched.
- Rules to specify both equipment to be carried and conduct.
- Certificate and often a badge are awarded for completion.
- Individual and team trophies are often awarded.
- Time limit allowing all but the slowest walkers to finish.
- Navigational ability essential.
- Results sheet is usually published.
- Essentially a challenge although a competitive element usually exists.

Official Long Distance Footpaths
- Officially designated by the Countryside Commission.
- Specific route.
- No time limit.
- Route is generally completed in several days of consecutive walking.
- Navigational ability is necessary.
- Route is waymarked with signposts and acorn symbols.
- Official guide usually available.

Recreational Footpaths

- Route instigated by voluntary bodies, local authorities or individuals.
- Route is along existing rights of way.
- No time limit.
- Completed either as a continuous exercise or in random sections.
- Published guide is available.
- Navigational ability is necessary.
- Not usually waymarked unless instigated by a local authority.

Format of Walk Descriptions

An illustrated summary of all the established long distance walks has been included. Each walk consists of the following sections where appropriate:

- Badge illustration – available to all those who successfully complete the walk.
- Key information – start, finish, distance, ascent, time limit and maps.
- Introduction – a brief description of the origin and characteristics of the walk.
- Completions – total number of completions recorded as at October 1981 plus the fastest recorded completion.
- Further information – sources of further details of routes and entry forms. Please ensure a stamped addressed envelope is enclosed. In some cases there may be a charge for leaflets. Prices and postages have not been included as these become rapidly outdated. Please enquire as to the price initially.
- References – these include all the published guides available and can usually be obtained through booksellers. In some cases an address has been provided. Please write for details of the price and postage enclosing a stamped addressed envelope.
- Route outline – shows the key points on the route, together with grid references, heights and progressive distances.
- Route log – in the case of open challenge walks and events a schedule is included showing the progressive time taken from the start usually at a 2½ m.p.h. pace. This can be adopted to your intended start time to allow you to compile your personal route schedule. The actual time of arrival can then be inserted in the log both to provide a permanent record and to monitor your progress. A typical route log might read as shown overleaf.
- Route map – this corresponds to the key points in the route outline. Maps are not drawn to a precise scale. A key to the map symbols used is shown overleaf.

INTRODUCTORY NOTES

- Route section – this corresponds both to the key points used in the route outline and on the route map.

In the case where annual challenge events are organised on the routes of open challenge walks, such as the Mallerstang Marathon and Three Peaks, they have been included in both sections. The route information has been shown under the open challenge walk with relevant details given in the appropriate section.

ROUTE OUTLINE

NO	GRID REF	CHECKPOINT	HEIGHT feet	DISTANCE mls	km
1	807 725	HORTON	790	.0	0
2	838 734	PEN-Y-GHENT	2273	2½	4
3	802 770	HIGH BIRKWITH	1100	6	10
4	764 792	RIBBLEHEAD	1000	9½	15
5	738 814	WHERNSIDE	2419	12	19
6	743 776	CHAPEL LE DALE	975	14½	23
7	742 746	INGLEBOROUGH	2373	17½	28
8	807 725	HORTON	790	22½	36

ROUTE LOG

2.5 MPH PACE	DATE 6.6.81.	DATE
0	8.00 am	
1.00	9.10	
2.25	10.30	
3.50	12.05 pm	
4.50	1.09	
5.50	2.15	
7.00	3.45	
9.00	5.55	
TOTAL TIME	9.55	

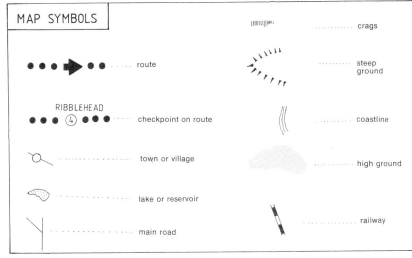

MAP SYMBOLS

●●●▶●● ..... route

RIBBLEHEAD
●●●④●●● ..... checkpoint on route

town or village

lake or reservoir

main road

crags

steep ground

coastline

high ground

railway

Open Challenge Walks

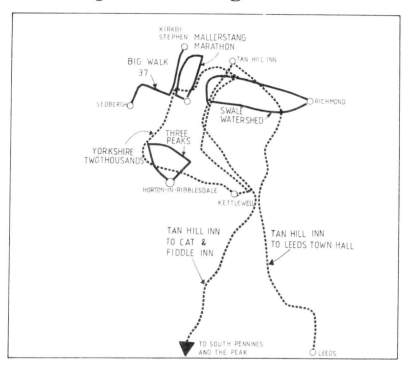

Three Peaks of Yorkshire	**22½ miles (36 km)**
Mallerstang Marathon	**25 miles (40 km)**
Swale Watershed Walk	**59 miles (94 km)**
Big Walk 37	**23 miles (37 km)**
Three Crags Walk	**15 miles (24 km)**

Ultra-Long Distance Challenges

Yorkshire Twothousands	**115 miles (185 km)**
Tan Hill Inn to Cat & Fiddle Inn	**120 miles (193 km)**
Tan Hill Inn to Leeds Town Hall	**85 miles (137 km)**

The Three Peaks of Yorkshire

Start and finish – Horton-in-Ribblesdale.

Distance – 22½ miles (36 km).
Time limit – 12 hours.

Ascent – 5,000 feet (1,524 m).

Maps – O.S. Sheet 98 (1:50,000); Three Peaks Outdoor Leisure map (1:25,000).

Introduction: An inspiring route taking in the first, second and seventh highest summits in North Yorkshire. It was first completed by the Yorkshire Rambling Club in 1897. The circuit has been a classic walk for some time and along with the Lyke Wake Walk, it is the most popular challenge in the country with thousands of completions each year. Regrettably the route has become eroded with heavy going and deep bog as much a characteristic of the walk as the panoramic views from the summits. An annual fell race (see page 37) and a cycle event are also staged on the route.

Completions: Total number of completions recorded – no information available. Fastest recorded completion – 2 hours 42 minutes by J. Norman (fell race route).

Further Information: Certificates and badges are available for successful circuits commencing at the Pen-y-Ghent Stores, Horton-in-Ribblesdale. Send a stamped addressed envelope to Mr P. Bayes, Pen-y-Ghent Stores, Horton-in-Ribblesdale, Yorkshire, BD24 0HE. 01729, 860333

References:
Walks in Limestone Country, A. Wainwright (Westmorland Gazette).
Three Peaks Footpath Map and Guide, Arthur Gemmell (Stile Publications, 1980, Mercury House, Otley, West Yorkshire, LS21 3HE.)
Yorkshire's Three Peaks (Dalesman Books, 1982)
The Big Walks, K. Wilson and R. Gilbert (Diadem Books, 1980).

THREE PEAKS OF YORKSHIRE

ROUTE OUTLINE

NO	GRID REF	CHECKPOINT	HEIGHT feet	DISTANCE mls	DISTANCE km
1	807 725	HORTON	790	0	0
2	838 734	PEN-Y-GHENT	2273	2½	4
3	802 770	HIGH BIRKWITH	1100	6	10
4	764 792	RIBBLEHEAD	1000	9½	15
5	738 814	WHERNSIDE	2419	12	19
6	743 776	CHAPEL LE DALE	975	14¼	23
7	742 746	INGLEBOROUGH	2373	17½	28
8	807 725	HORTON	790	22½	36

ROUTE LOG

2.5 MPH PACE	DATE –	DATE –
0		
1.00		
2.25		
3.50		
4.50		
5.50		
7.00		
9.00		
TOTAL TIME		

ROUTE SECTION

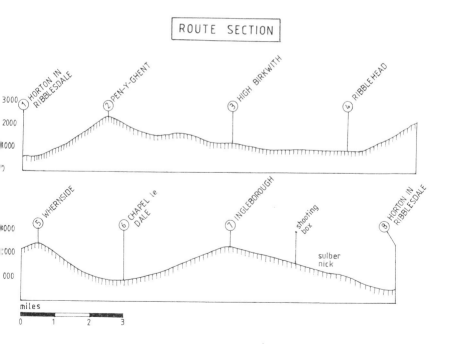

13

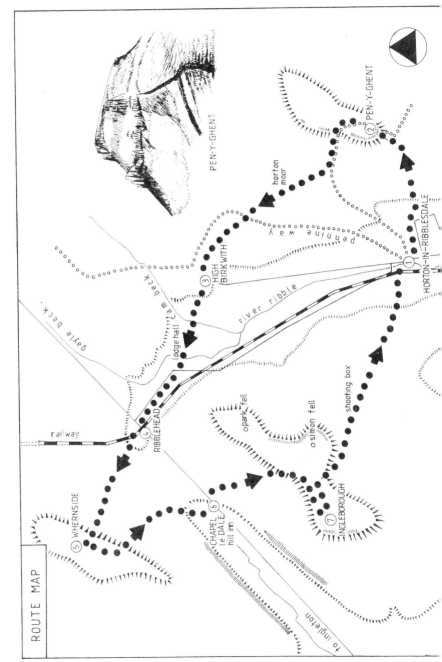

ROUTE MAP

PEN-Y-GHENT

14

The Mallerstang Marathon

Start and finish – Garsdale Head Youth Hostel.
Distance – 25 miles (40 km)   **Ascent – 4,000 feet (1,220 m)**
Time limit – 12 hours.
Maps – O.S. Sheets 91, 98 (1:50,000).

Introduction: A fine walk over the wild fells of the North Yorkshire–Cumbria border devised by Philip Gilks on behalf of the Youth Hostels Association in 1972. The walk is based on Garsdale Head Youth Hostel, the highest hostel in Yorkshire splendidly situated 1,250 feet up on the slopes of Lunds Fell near the sources of the rivers Ure and Eden. Rough terrain, magnificent views of the Pennines, Howgills and Lake District mountains combine with the solitude of this wild country to make a memorable and rewarding day out.

Completions: No records maintained.

Further Information: Badges are not available except to those participating in the annual event; certificates for the route are only awarded to participants who stay at the hostel. For details of the route send a stamped addressed envelope to The Warden, Garsdale Head Youth Hostel, Shaws, Lunds, Sedbergh, Cumbria, LA10 5PY.

Challenge Event: An organised event on this route also takes place annually (see page 36 for details).

| \multicolumn{5}{c}{ROUTE OUTLINE} | \multicolumn{3}{c}{ROUTE LOG} |

NO	GRID REF	CHECKPOINT	HEIGHT feet	DISTANCE mls	km	2.5 MPH PACE	DATE –	DATE –
1	796 948	GARSDALE HEAD YH	1250	0	0	0		
2	802 013	HIGH SEAT	2328	5	8	2.00		
3	825 061	NINE STANDARDS RIGG	2171	9½	15	3.50		
4	803 054	TAILBRIDGE HILL	1796	11½	18	4.35		
5	782 042	DALEFOOT	722	14	22	5.35		
6	758 988	WILDBOAR FELL	2324	19	30	7.35		
7	781 941	TURNER HILL	1525	23	37	9.10		
8	796 948	GARSDALE HEAD YH	1250	25	40	10.10		
						TOTAL TIME		

MALLERSTANG MARATHON

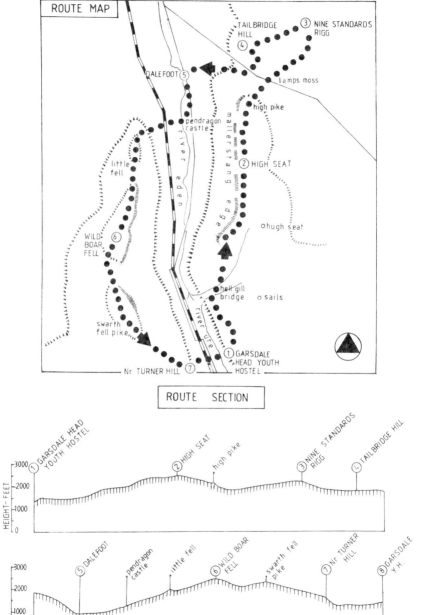

ROUTE MAP

ROUTE SECTION

The Swale Watershed Walk

Start and finish – Richmond.
Distance – 59 miles (94 km).
Ascent – 5,650 feet (1,722 m).
Time limit – 48 hours.
Maps – O.S. Sheets 92, 98, 99,
  (1:50,000).

Introduction: This walk was originated in 1970 by members of the Swale Outdoor Centre as a weekend expedition to be attempted only between November and March. Navigational expertise is extremely important as most of the walk is over remote, rough, undefined terrain. The severity of the route should not be underestimated and it is strongly advised that only those with several years experience of challenge walks attempt this route.

Completions: Total number of recorded completions – 63. Fastest recorded completion – 20 hours 30 minutes jointly recorded by M.

ROUTE OUTLINE						ROUTE LOG	
NO	GRID REF	CHECKPOINT	HEIGHT feet	DISTANCE mls	km	2.5 MPH PACE	DATE
1	169 006	RICHMOND	300	0	0	0	
2	105 006	MARSKE	550	6	9	2.25	
3	074 028	HELWITH	800	10	16	4.00	
4	005 025	LANGTHWAITE	850	16	25	6.25	
5	947 024	FRIARFOLD MOOR	1931	20	32	8.00	
6	898 039	BLACK MOOR	1855	24	39	9.35	
7	849 018	BIRKDALE TARN	1600	28	45	11.10	
8	848 973	GREAT SHUNNER FELL	2340	32	50	12.50	
9	937 944	OXNOP BECK HEAD	1600	39	62	15.35	
10	028 957	GREETS HILL	1676	46	73	18.25	
11	073 946	PRESTON MOOR	1250	49	78	19.35	
12	104 965	STAINTON	700	52	83	20.50	
13	112 978	DOWN HOLME	700	53	85	21.15	
14	143 003	HUDSWELL	725	56	89	22.25	
15	169 006	RICHMOND	300	59	94	23.35	

TOTAL TIME ⟩

SWALE WATERSHED WALK

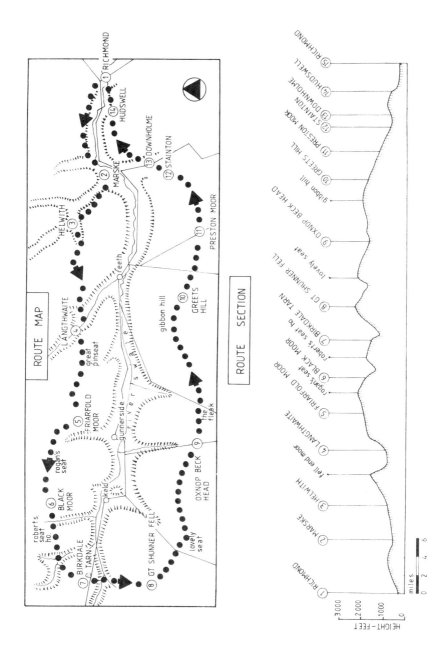

ROUTE MAP

ROUTE SECTION

Greaves, E. Bishop, M. Powell-Davies, C. Dodd, F. Thomas and M. Grimley.

Further Information: Send a stamped addressed envelope for details of the route, badge and certificate to Stuart Pailor, High Springwell House, Hart, Hartlepool, Cleveland.

Big Walk 37 –
Wild Boar Fell and the Howgills

Start – Kirkby Stephen (Grid reference 775 086).
Finish – Sedbergh (Grid reference 657 922).
Distance – 23 miles (37 km).
Time limit – None.
Maps – O.S. sheets 91, 97, 98 (1:50,000).

Origin: R. Gilbert, 1980.

Description: *The Big Walks* is perhaps the most inspiring and exhilarating collection of photographs and walks on the British

Evening light on the Howgills (*Geoffrey N. Wright*).

19

mountains ever to be compiled. Fifty-five routes are included, ten of which are in England. Two of these fall within the Yorkshire Dales region, the classic Three Peaks and this walk in the less frequented area of Wild Boar Fell and the Howgills. Starting from Kirkby Stephen the walk climbs the western edge of the Eden valley over Little Fell, the Nab, Wild Boar Fell and Swarth Pike Fell where it turns westwards to Ulldale and Rawthey Bridge. The route then continues along the river Rawthey for a short way before ascending by the impressive waterfall of Cautley Spout to the Calf. Easy undulating walking then leads to Sedbergh.

Reference: *The Big Walks*, K. Wilson and R. Gilbert (Diadem Books, 1980).

The Three Crags Walk

Start – Weeton station (Grid reference 276 476).
Finish – Ben Rhydding station (Grid reference 134 477).
Distance – 15 miles (24 km).
Time Limit – None.
Maps – O.S. Sheet 104 (1:50,000).

Origin: Lower Wharfedale R.A. Group, 1978.

Description: A pleasant undemanding walk in lower Wharfedale from Almscliffe Crag to Ilkley's Cow and Calf via Caley Crags on Otley Chevin. The walk does not reach the 20 miles long distance qualification but it does make a good practice route in preparation for longer marathons such as the Three Peaks. The walk could be extended by returning to the start point to make a circuit of over 20 miles.

Further Information: For details of the route description and badge send a stamped addressed envelope to C. Newton, Lower Wharfedale R.A. Group, 23 Hall Drive, Burley-in-Wharfedale, Ilkley, West Yorkshire LS29 7LR.

Ultra-Long Distance Challenges
Yorkshire Twothousands

Start and finish – Kettlewell. **Distance – 115 miles (185 km)**
Summits – 26. **Ascent – 19,368 feet.**
Time limit – To be determined.

Origin: Peter Barker, West Yorkshire Long Distance Walkers' Association, 1980.

Description: Although the advent of metrication has abolished feet from the map no doubt the lure of the 2,000 foot mountains of England will continue to inspire and challenge walkers for a good time yet. Certainly this circuit of 26 mountains (as defined by George Bridge) within the new Yorkshire boundaries represents one of the most formidable treks devised for the ultra-long distance walker and runner. Comparison with the Lakeland Bob Graham Round of 42 summits, 72 miles and 27,000 feet of ascent is inevitable and what is lost in climbing is more than made up for in distance and arduous terrain. A walk designed for the elite, those dedicated few who have acquired the ability to tolerate the highest levels of mental and physical self-abuse!

Further Information: Send a stamped addressed envelope for details to Peter Barker, 179 Forest Lane, Harrogate, HG2 7EQ.

Reference: *The Mountains of England and Wales*, George Bridge (West Col Publications, 1973), Gaston's Alpine Books, Goring, Reading, Berkshire, RG8 0AP.

INGLEBOROUGH

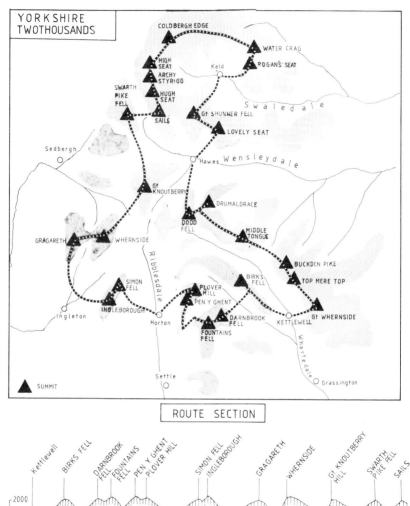

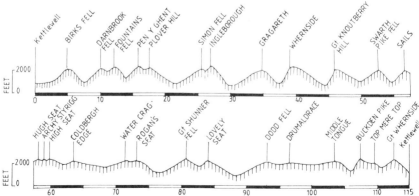

ROUTE OUTLINE						LOG
SUMMIT	GRID REF	ROUTE	HEIGHT feet	DISTANCE miles	ASCENT feet	DATE –
–	968 723	Kettlewell	–	0	0	
1	919 764	BIRKS FELL	2,001	5.0	1,300	✓
2	885 728	DARNBROOK FELL	2,048	10.3	2,512	✓
3	864 716	FOUNTAINS FELL	2,191	11.9	2,803	✓
4	839 734	PEN-Y-GHENT	2,273	15.7	3,686	✓
5	849 752	PLOVER HILL	2,231	17.3	3,917	✓
6	754 752	SIMON FELL	2,100	25.8	5,317	
7	741 746	INGLEBOROUGH	2,378	26.9	5,695	
8	691 795	GRAGARETH	2,050	34.7	7,095	
9	738 814	WHERNSIDE	2,419	38.9	8,015	
10	788 872	Gt KNOUTBERRY HILL	2,203	45.7	9,738	
11	762 956	SWARTH PIKE FELL	2,125	52.4	10,838	
12	808 966	SAILS	2,186	56.3	11,878	
13	809 991	HUGH SEAT	2,257	58.1	12,135	
14	803 003	ARCHY STYRIGG	2,250	59.1	12,235	
15	802 013	HIGH SEAT	2,328	59.8	12,413	
16	828 053	COLDBERGH EDGE	2,175	63.6	12,913	
17	928 046	WATER CRAG	2,188	71.6	13,663	
18	919 031	ROGAN'S SEAT	2,203	73.0	13,817	
19	849 973	Gt SHUNNER FELL	2,340	80.8	15,117	
20	879 951	LOVELY SEAT	2,213	84.0	15,607	
21	841 846	DODD FELL HILL	2,189	93.2	17,007	
22	874 867	DRUMALDRALE	2,015	96.5	17,247	
23	909 811	MIDDLE TONGUE	2,109	103.5	17,682	
24	961 788	BUCKDEN PIKE	2,302	107.5	18,608	✓
25	969 765	TOP MERE TOP	2,050	109.5	18,658	
26	002 739	Gt WHERNSIDE	2,310	112.5	19,368	
–	968 723	Kettlewell	–	115.0	–	

TOTAL TIME

Tan Hill Inn to Cat & Fiddle Inn

Start – Tan Hill Inn, 1732 feet, County Durham (Grid reference 897 067).
Finish – Cat & Fiddle Inn, 1690 feet, Cheshire (Grid reference 001 719).
Distance – 120 miles (193 km).
Ascent –19,450 feet (5,928 m).
Maps – O.S. Sheets 91, 98, 104, 110, 119.

Origin: Fred Heardman, Rucksack Club, 1952.

Description: The Rucksack Club founded in 1902 was the first to specialise in long distance walks, a tradition which exists to the present day. This outing, a pub crawl down the backbone of the Pennines connecting England's two highest inns, was devised in 1952 to celebrate the Silver Jubilee of that year. The route was carefully chosen and although minor variations are permitted it should include Great Shunner Fell, Hawes, Marsett, Buckden Pike, Great Whernside, Grassington, Rylstone Fell, Skipton, Cowling, Wolf Stones, Boulsworth Hill, Jackson's Ridge, Widdup Reservoir, Todmorden, Blackstone Edge, Marsden, Black Hill, Bleaklow, Kinder Scout, Edale, Chapel Gate and Long Hill. Although among the severest tests of stamina to be contemplated, crossings by the Rucksackers have become quite common, such that only winter crossings are now regarded with any real esteem!

Completions: Originally completed by V. J. Desmond in 54 hours 10 minutes and Messrs. Williamson and Courtenay in 55 hours 40 minutes. Fastest recorded completion by M. Cudahy in 32 hours 20 minutes.

Reference: *High Peak,* Byne and Sutton (Secker and Warburg, 1966).

Tan Hill Inn to Leeds Town Hall

Start – Tan Hill Inn, County Durham (Grid reference 897 067).
Finish – Leeds Town Hall, West Yorkshire (Grid reference 297 339).
Distance – 85 miles (137 km).
Ascent – 5,000 feet (1,524 m).
Maps – O.S. Sheets 91, 98, 99, 104.

Origin: West Yorkshire Long Distance Walkers' Association, 1979.

Description: Inspired by the Rucksack Club's infamous Tan–Cat epic, the 85 mile route is made up of three distinct sections – the traverse of Swaledale, Wensleydale and Coverdale to Great Whernside via Long Row, Castle Bolton and Bradley; a tough high level section of undefined country above Wharfedale to Stump Cross Cavern and onto Ilkley via Beamsley Beacon; and the final section following the Dales Way Link to Leeds taking in Eccup Reservoir and Hustlers Row before crossing Woodhouse Moor to the Town Hall.

Completions: Messrs Barker, Bell, Towers and Wimbush in 30 hours 55 minutes, October 1979.

Challenge Events

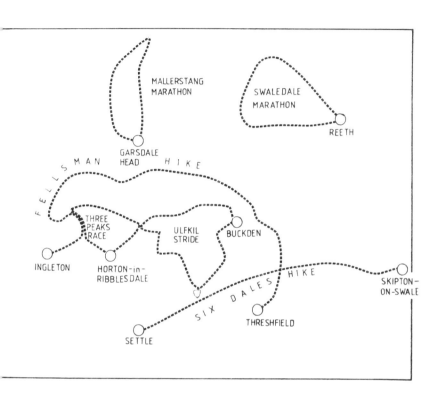

Fellsman Hike	**60 miles (96 km)**
Six Dales Hike	**42 miles (67 km)**
Swaledale Marathon	**23 miles (37 km)**
Ulfkil Stride	**33 miles (53 km)**
Mallerstang Marathon	**25 miles (40 km)**
Three Peaks Race	**23 miles (36 km)**

The Fellsman Hike

Start – Ingleton.
Finish –Threshfield.
Distance – **60 miles (96 km)**.
Ascent – **11,100 feet (3,385 m)**.
Time limit – **Restricted by checkpoint deadlines.**
Map – **O.S. Sheet 98 (1:50,000).**

Introduction: First promoted in 1962 by the Keighley Scout Service Team this was the first challenge event to be organised in the North of England. This has undoubtedly set both the scene and standard for all those events that have followed. Since those early days when there were only 57 starters and 15 finishers with a fastest time of 23 hours 20 minutes recorded jointly by Messrs Howe and Roulson, the hike has grown to be one of the most prestigious events on the calendar with an annual draw now being made for the 450 places. The highest standards of organisation, communications and safety are maintained throughout the event.

Long since regarded as one of the classic tests in challenge walking the course offers a relentless horseshoe of peak and bog including the notorious night-time traverse of Fleetmoss. Everyone who participates in the hike receives a commemorative tally specially designed by Colin Mear of Connersville Ramblers which has become a hallmark of the hike. A distinctive badge and certificate are available to all successful competitors.

The full list of trophies is as follows:

Fellsman Axe	– Fastest individual
Jim Nelson Trophy	– Fastest lady
Tregoning Cup	– Fastest novice (first time of entry)
Levy Trophy	– Fastest scout/scout leader
Service Trophy	– Fastest club (first three members)
Fellsman Shield	– Fastest scout group (first three members)

Note: Many parts of the Fellsman route are on private land for which permission to pass is given *only* on the day of the event. Please do not trespass and jeopardise the future of this event.

Completions: Fastest recorded completion – 11 hours 44 minutes by A. Richardson.

Further Information: Send a large stamped addressed envelope for details of future events to Fellsman Hike, P.O. Box 30, Keighley, West Yorkshire.

	ROUTE OUTLINE					ROUTE LOG		
GRID REF	CHECKPOINT	HEIGHT feet	DISTANCE mls	km	2.5 MPH PACE	DATE –	DATE –
695 730	INGLETON	450	0	0	0		
741 745	INGLEBOROUGH	2373	3½	6	1.25		
744 777	HILL INN	975	6½	10	2.35		
738 814	WHERNSIDE	2419	9	14	3.35		
706 791	KINGSDALE	975	12½	20	5.00		
688 793	GRAGARETH	2057	14	22	5.35		
699 836	GREAT COUM	2250	17	27	6.50		
698 859	FLINTERGILL	1150	18½	30	7.25		
724 859	WHERNSIDE MANOR	550	21	34	8.25		
773 826	BLEA MOOR	1753	25	40	10.00		
770 860	STONEHOUSE	831	27½	44	11.00		
789 872	GREAT KNOUTBERRY	2203	30	48	12.00		
797 843	REDSHAW	1434	32	51	12.50		
809 842	SNAIZEHOLME	1650	33	53	13.10		
841 846	DODD FELL	2189	35½	57	14.10		
860 838	FLEET MOSS	1910	37	59	14.50		
909 811	MIDDLE TONGUE	2109	41½	66	16.35		
943 805	CRAY	1376	44	70	17.35		
961 788	BUCKDEN PIKE	2302	46	74	18.25		
965 753	TOP MERE	1600	48½	78	19.25		
987 757	PARK RASH	1624	50	80	20.00		
002 739	GREAT WHERNSIDE	2310	52	83	20.50		
997 686	KELBER	1200	55½	89	22.10		
015 659	YARNBURY	1150	58	93	23.10		
993 639	THRESHFIELD	610	60	96	24.00		
					TOTAL TIME		

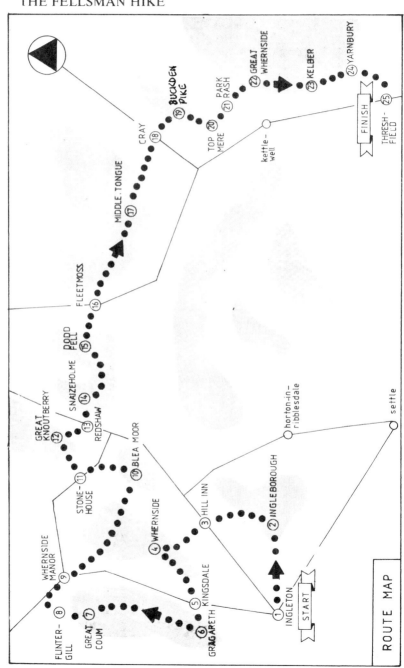

ROUTE MAP

THE FELLSMAN HIKE

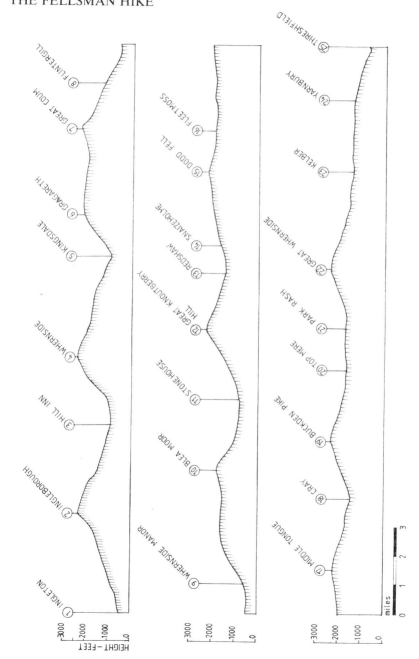

HEIGHT—FEET

3000
2000
1000
0

① INGLETON
② INGLEBOROUGH
③ HILL INN
④ WHERNSIDE
⑤ KINGSDALE
⑥ GRAGARETH
⑦ GREAT COUM
⑧ FLINTERGILL

⑨ WHERNSIDE MANOR
⑩ BLEA MOOR
⑪ STONE HOUSE
⑫ GREAT KNOUTBERRY HILL
⑬ REDSHAW
⑭ SNAIZEHOLME
⑮ DODD FELL
⑯ FLEET MOSS

⑰ MIDDLE TONGUE
⑱ CRAY
⑲ BUCKDEN PIKE
⑳ TOP MERE
㉑ PARK RASH
㉒ GREAT WHERNSIDE
㉓ KELBER
㉔ YARNBURY
㉕ THRESHFIELD

miles
0   1   2   3

29

The Six Dales Hike

Start – Settle.
Distance – 42 miles (67 km).
Maps – O.S. Sheets 98 and 99 (1:50,000).
Time limit – Restricted by checkpoint deadlines.

Finish – Skipton-on-Swaledale.
Ascent – 3,000 feet (914 m).

Introduction: This challenge event was pioneered in 1956 by the North-West Leeds Scout District and takes place each September. Although the event is restricted to members of the Scout and Guide Movement in Yorkshire the route may be undertaken at any time by any long distance walker as it is entirely on rights of way. It may therefore be enjoyed as an anytime challenge within a self-imposed time limit or as a casual walk over a number of days. As its name suggests the walk crosses six dales – Ribblesdale, Airedale, Wharfedale, Nidderdale, Wensleydale and Swaledale. A variety of scenery and walking is encountered, including the limestone country of Settle and Malham, the moors above Conistone and Grewelthorpe, the picturesque village of West Tanfield and the agricultural landscape of the Vale of York.

A number of individual and team trophies are available to male and female participants according to age. Badges are not issued.

ROUTE OUTLINE						ROUTE LOG		
NO	GRID REF	CHECKPOINT	HEIGHT feet	DISTANCE mls	km	2.5 MPH PACE	DATE –	DATE –
1	820 636	SETTLE	500	0	0	0		
2	905 657	STREET GATE	1300	6	10	2.25		
3	975 678	KILNSEY	600	11	18	4.25		
4	020 700	MOSSDALE BECK	1450	15	24	6.00		
5	057 729	HOW STEAN BECK	1100	18	29	7.10		
6	091 741	MIDDLESMOOR	900	20	32	8.00		
7	120 751	OUSTER BECK	1400	23	37	9.10		
8	173 761	GREWELTHORPE MOOR	1050	27	44	10.50		
9	230 763	GREWELTHORPE	500	31	50	12.25		
10	269 789	WEST TANFIELD	150	34	54	13.35		
11	325 771	WATH	100	38	61	15.10		
12	366 799	SKIPTON ON SWALE	100	42	67	16.50		
						TOTAL TIME		

SIX DALES HIKE

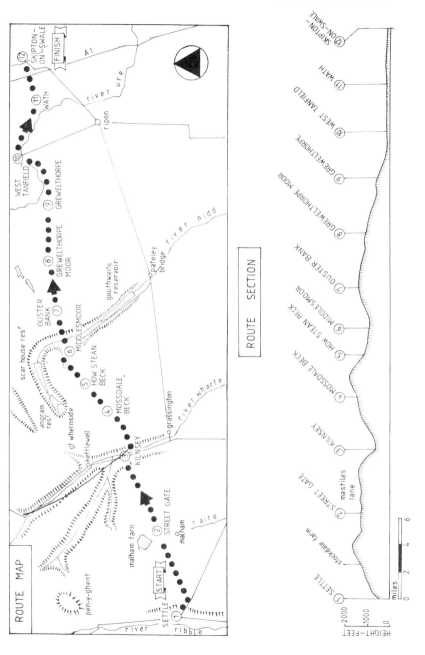

ROUTE MAP

ROUTE SECTION

31

Completions: Fastest recorded completion is 8 hours 1 minute by Airedale Scout Fellowship.

Further Information: Entry forms (for Yorkshire Scouts and Guides) are available by sending a stamped addressed envelope to David Boulton, 23 Otley Old Road, Leeds, LS16 6HB. For a route description of the walk send a stamped addressed envelope to D. Burland, 26 Nursery Road, Guiseley, Leeds.

The Swaledale Marathon

Start and Finish – Reeth.
Distance – **23 miles (37 km).**
Ascent – **3,000 feet (915 m).**
Time limit – **10 hours.**
Maps – **O.S. Sheets 92, 98 (1:50,000).**

Introduction: Originated in 1979, the event is now staged each June by the Swaledale Outdoor Club. Varied walking and scenery including Fremington Edge, Arkengarthdale and Swaledale itself make this into a popular and attractive event. The Surrender Bridge checkpoint is notable for featuring in the credits of the television series 'All Creatures Great and Small' based on the popular James

		ROUTE OUTLINE				ROUTE LOG		
NO	GRID REF	CHECKPOINT	HEIGHT feet	DISTANCE mls	km	2.5 MPH PACE	DATE –	DATE –
1	038 993	REETH	600	0	0	0		
2	999 036	ARKLE BECK BRIDGE	900	5	8	2.00		
3	946 043	LEVEL	1750	9	15	3.35		
4	963 014	LEVEL HOUSE	1500	11½	18	4.35		
5	947 015	GUNNERSIDE GILL	1850	13	21	5.15		
6	951 982	GUNNERSIDE	750	16	25	6.25		
7	988 999	SURRENDER BRIDGE	1150	19	30	7.40		
8	038 993	REETH	600	23	37	9.15		
						TOTAL TIME		

SWALEDALE MARATHON

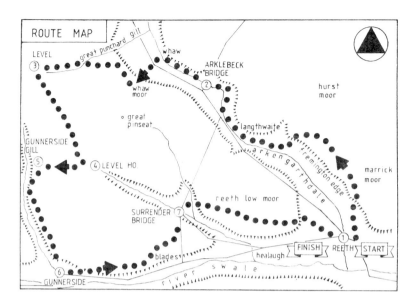

ROUTE MAP

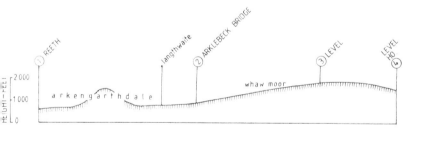

ROUTE SECTION

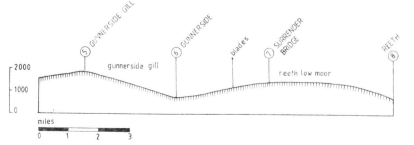

Herriot novels. A badge and certificate are available to all successful participants.

Completions: The fastest recorded time is 3 hours 15 minutes by D. Weir.

Further Information: For information on future events send a large stamped addressed envelope to Stuart Pailor, High Springwell House, Hart, Hartlepool, Cleveland.

The Ulfkil Stride

Start and finish – Buckden.
Distance – 33 miles (53 km),
              – 24 miles (38 km).
Ascent – 15,000 feet (1,524 m).
              – 3,500 feet (1,068 m).
Maps – O.S. Sheet 98 (1:50,000);
Malhamdale and Upper Wharfedale Outdoor Leisure Map (1:25,000).
Time limit – 11 hours.

Introduction: A walk representing one of the most scenic and rewarding days out in the fells of northern England. First organised by the West Yorkshire Group of the Long Distance Walkers' Association in 1979, this dual distance event is now held each June. The Ulfkil Cross (located close to Dalehead at grid reference 842 715) on the ancient monastic boundary of Fountains Abbey gives its name to the course, which includes the steep ascents and extensive views from Horse Head Pass, Pen-y-Ghent, Fountains Fell and Old Cote Moor.

Jack Rayner devised this impressive route and following his death in 1980 a Jack Rayner Trophy is awarded to the first super-veteran (over 50 years) to complete the full route. Certificates and badges are available to all participants who complete the course within 11 hours.

Completions: Fastest recorded time is 5 hours 26 minutes by D. Calder.

Further Information: An entry form and details are obtainable from January prior to each event by sending a stamped addressed envelope to Peter Barker, 179 Forest Lane, Harrogate, North Yorkshire, HG2 7EQ.

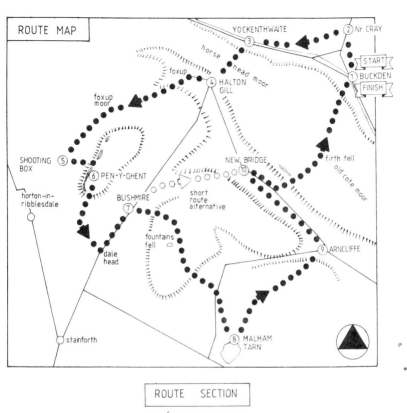

ROUTE MAP

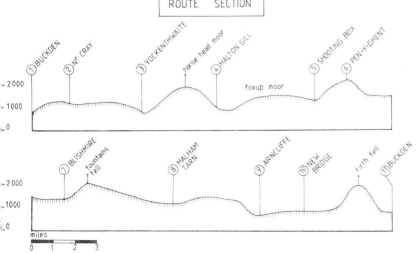

ROUTE SECTION

ROUTE OUTLINE					
NO	GRID REF	CHECKPOINT	HEIGHT feet	DISTANCE mls	km
1	943 773	BUCKDEN	800	0	0
2	945 797	Nr CRAY	1200	2	3
3	904 790	YOCKENTHWAITE	800	5	8
4	879 767	HALTON GILL	1000	8	13
5	823 743	SHOOTING BOX	1250	13	21
6	838 734	PEN-Y-GHENT	2273	14	22
7	853 723	BLISHMIRE	1400	18	29
8	897 671	MALHAM TARN	1250	23	37
9	931 719	ARNCLIFFE	750	27	44
10	898 742	NEW BRIDGE	800	29	46
11	943 773	BUCKDEN	800	33	53

ROUTE LOG		
3.0 MPH PACE	DATE -	DATE -
0		
35		
1.35		
2.35		
4.20		
4.40		
6.00		
7.35		
9.00		
9.35		
11.00		
TOTAL TIME		

The Mallerstang Marathon Event

Description: An event based on the open, anytime challenge route (see page 15 for details) and first staged in July 1972. It was held annually until 1977 and then revived in 1981 by the Leeds group of the Youth Hostels Association with the introduction of a badge for successful participants.

Completions: The fastest recorded completion is 5 hours 8 minutes by I. Ferguson (records commenced 1981).

Further Information: For details of future events send a large stamped addressed envelope to M. Boldison, 6 Westbourne Avenue, Garforth, Leeds, LS25 1BU.

The Three Peaks Race

Description: Now in its twenty-eighth year (1981) and organised by the Three Peaks Race Association with the Sponsorship of the *Daily Mirror* newspaper under the rules of A.A.A. As one of the most prestigious races on the fell running calendar the number of entries is such that a ballot is held for all but the first 200 places. All entries are strictly vetted.

A number of trophies are awarded as follows:

N. Thornber trophy   – individual winner
Daily Mirror trophy   – first team
S. Bradshaw trophy   – first veteran
P. Wandsworth trophy   – first man representing a Yorkshire club.

There are also a number of prizes specifically for ladies. Certificates are awarded to all successful competitors.

Completions: Fastest recorded completion by J. Norman in 2 hours 42 minutes.

Further Information: Send a stamped addressed envelope for entry form for future events from J. K. Windle, 2 Langholme Close, Barrowford, Nelson, Lancashire.

PENYGHENT FROM
HULL POT
(TOM PARKER)

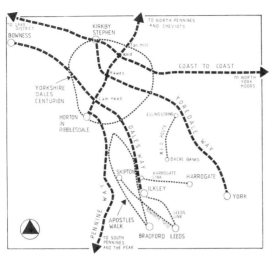

Official Lon Distance Footpaths and Recreational Footpaths

Official Long Distance Footpaths

Pennine Way	270 miles (432 km)

Recreational Footpaths

Apostles Walk	80 miles (129 km)
Abbott's Hike	106 miles (171 km)
R. E. D. Route	25 miles (40 km)
Coast to Coast	190 miles (306 km)
Dales Way	81 miles (130 km)
Harrogate Dales Way Link	20 miles (32 km)
Leeds Dales Way Link	20 miles (32 km)
Towpath Trod	29 miles (46 km)
Yoredale Way	100 miles (161 km)
Yorkshire Dales Centurion Walk	100 miles (161 km)
Coast to Coast II	120 miles (193 km)
Harrogate Inner Ring (proposed)	20 miles (32 km)

Why do I go
Through rain, wind and snow
Walking east, walking west
On an unending quest?
Over the rock-scarred shoulder
Where the fells fling up boulders:
Past the high cairns where the curlews cry
To the daemon-haunted sky;
Over the whams and the hags
To the ultimate crags!

This only I know
I must go
A spirit bids me to go
Over the moors and fells
Where the kestrel dwells,
To the high places of the world
Where the four winds are hurled
I take my stand alone
Where the eagles moan,
There is a fever in the blood
Craving for solitude.

When I am old and full of pains
I will sit at home and count my gains:
The peaks I've climbed: the ridges won:
I will number them carefully one by one.
And take a tally of all the dales
Where I have heard the shepherds' tales;
I will count the sikes and becks and ghylls
I've followed to their guardian hills;
And dream of bathes in lonely tarns
On mountain tops on summer morns,
When I am old and cannot roam
Far from home . . .
But time enough to do all this
When I have lost youth's ectasies.

'Wanderlust',
Alfred J. Brown, 1948

The Pennine Way

Start – Edale, Derbyshire.   Finish – Kirk Yetholm, Borders
Distance – 270 miles (432 km).   Region.
Ascent – 27,000 feet (7,925 m).
Maps – O.S. Sheets 74, 80, 86, 91, 92, 98, 103, 109, 110 (1:50,000).
Links – Peak and South Pennines: Peakland Way, Calderdale Way.
      Yorkshire Dales: Dales Way, Yoredale Way, Centurion
      Walk, Coast to Coast, Pennine Link.
      North Pennines and Cheviots: Hadrians Wall Walk, Reivers
      Way.

Introduction: The Pennine Way has captured the imagination of thousands and inspired people of all ages and backgrounds to don boots and rucksacks and take up the gauntlet; many have succeeded and many more have failed! Whatever the outcome there is no question that it is an unforgettable experience; a journey along the backbone of England; a tapestry of people, places, memories, scenes, challenges and rewards. Although officially opened on April 24, 1965, as Britain's first long distance footpath, the concept first appeared as an article by Tom Stephenson in the *Daily Herald* on June 23, 1935. It then took 30 years of campaigning, battling with authority and the provision of the 1949 National Parks and Access to the Countryside Act before the route became a reality.

The trek commences with the peat groughs of Kinder and Bleaklow followed by the wild moorland of the Bronte country before reaching the superb limestone scenery of the Yorkshire Dales. Streams disappear underground and potholes abound as the walk passes Malham Tarn and Cove and makes the ascent of Pen-y-Ghent to descend to Horton-in-Ribblesdale. From here good tracks lead over to Hawes in Wensleydale. Great Shunner Fell is climbed on the way to Swaledale and the lonely Tan Hill Inn. Once an important meeting place of trade routes and the haunt of coal miners this is a welcome stop and has the distinction of being England's highest pub at 1,732 feet. The Way continues to Teesdale and the impressive waterfalls of High Force and Cauldron Snout and to High Cup Nick, Dufton and Cross Fell, the highest point on the walk. The route carries on through the Northumberland National Park to Hadrian's Wall, Kielder Forest and the Cheviot Hills and over the border into Scotland descending to Kirk Yetholm. At one time a free pint at the Border Hotel, courtesy of Alfred Wainwright who wrote the *Pennine Way Companion,* awaited successful walkers but you will now have to buy your own!

The popularity of the Pennine Way should not disguise the difficulties involved and the need for thorough planning and preparation cannot be over emphasised. Prospective wayfarers should be skilled with map and compass and should have developed the necessary stamina to walk on consecutive days. Within two miles of the start at Edale are conditions which in bad weather can stretch the navigational expertise and stamina of the most experienced walker.

Completions: Fastest recorded completion – Brian Harney in 3 days and 42 minutes. This remarkable run which currently features in the *Guinness Book of Records* started at 9 a.m. on August 9, 1979, at Kirk Yetholm and finished at 9.42 a.m. at Edale on August 12, 1979. On the first day Brian, a member of Dark Peak Fell Runners and Rotherham Harriers, completed 113 miles, 81 miles on the second, 74 miles on the third and two miles on the fourth!

Further Information: Badges and certificates are not issued. Pennine Way Council – Exists to secure the protection of the Way and provide information to the public. In association with the Countryside Commission the Council publishes an accommodation

ROUTE OUTLINE

NO	GRID REF	LOCATION	HEIGHT feet	DISTANCE mls	km
1	123 859	EDALE	800	0	0
2	055 986	CROWDEN	725	15	24
3	018 095	STANDEDGE	1250	26	42
4	972 265	HEBDEN BRIDGE	425	42	67
5	966 428	COWLING	670	58	93
6	932 541	GARGRAVE	375	70	112
7	901 629	MALHAM	650	77	123
8	809 724	HORTON-IN-RIBBLESDALE	775	92	147
9	873 898	HAWES	800	107	171
10	893 012	KELD	1050	120	192
11	933 183	BLACKTON BRIDGE	950	135	216
12	947 254	MIDDLETON-IN-TEESDALE	750	141	226
13	854 302	SAUR HILL	1200	149	238
14	690 250	DUFTON	600	162	259
15	745 415	GARRIGILL	1124	179	286
16	717 462	ALSTON	900	183	292
	657 659	THIRLWALL	450	200	320
	751 676	PEEL ROAD	900	207	331
	839 833	BELLINGHAM	378	225	360
	771 024	BYRNESS	750	241	385
	827 282	KIRK YETHOLM	350	270	432

ROUTE LOG

DATE	TIME

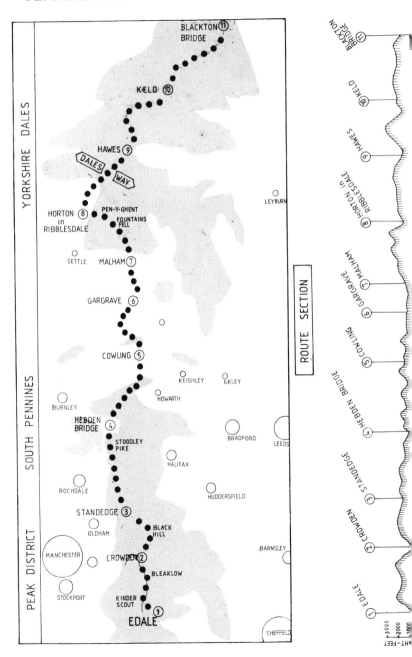

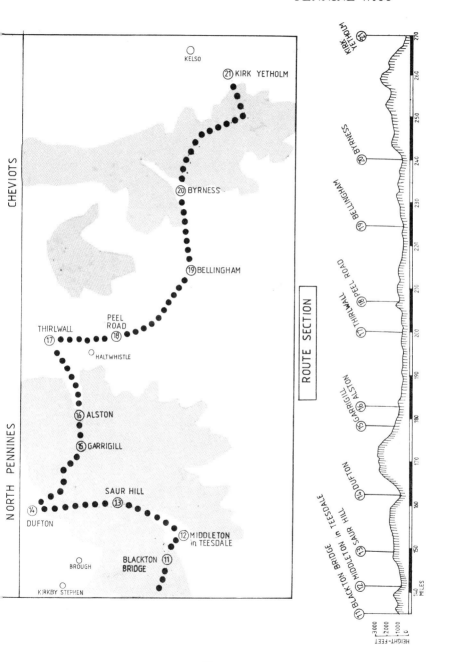

list. A newsletter is published twice a year. For membership details send a stamped addressed envelope to Mr R. Smith, 236 Lidgett Lane, Leeds LS17 6QH. For details of the accommodation list see references below.

References:
Pennine Way Companion, A. Wainwright (Westmorland Gazette, 1976).
The Pennine Way, K. Oldham (Dalesman, 1969).
A Guide to the Pennine Way, C. J. Wright (Constable, 1977).
Walking the Pennine Way, A. Binns (Warne Gerrard, 1966).
A Walker on the Pennine Way, C. Walker (Pendyke, 1977).
The Pennine Way Pub Guide, Jowett, Mellor, Wilson. Send stamped addressed envelope for details to P. Wilson, 76 Colne Lane, Colne, Lancashire.
The Pennine Way, T. Stephenson (Ramblers' Association). Send stamped addressed envelope for details to Ramblers' Association, 1/5 Wandsworth Road, London, SW8 2LJ.
Pennine Way Accommodation List, (Pennine Way Council). Send stamped addressed envelope for details to J. Needham, 23 Woodland Crescent, Hulton Park, Prestwich, Manchester, M25 8WQ.
High Peak, Byne and Sutton (Secker and Warburg, 1966).

The Apostles Walk

Start – Harden (Grid reference 086 384).
Finish – Wilsden (Grid reference 092 366).
Distance – 80 miles (129 km).
Maps – O.S. Sheets 98, 103, 104.

Origin: Devised by A. T. Ashworth, A. Valters and the Vicar of Harden and Wilsden in 1974 to raise church funds.

Description: A walk from the outskirts of Bradford to the southern part of the Dales visiting the twelve churches of St. Thomas, Sutton-in-Craven; St. Andrew, Kildwick; St. Margaret, Ilkley: Bolton Abbey; St. Winifred, Burnsall; St. Oswald, Arncliffe; St. Michael, Malham; St. Peter, Coniston Cold; St. Andrew, Gargrave; Holy Trinity, Skipton; St. Stephen, Kildwick and finishing at St. Matthew's at Wilsden. The route indicates the infinite variety of long distance walks which can be devised even from an industrial area.

Completions: Total number of completions recorded – 10.

Further Information: Send a stamped addressed envelope for a route description and details of the colourful badge to Mr A. T. Ashworth, 22 Lane Side, Haworth Road, Wilsden, Bradford, BD15 0LH.

Abbott's Hike

Start – Ilkley (Grid reference 117 476).
Finish – Pooley Bridge, Penrith (Grid reference 470 244).
Distance – 106 miles (171 km).
Maps – O.S. Sheets 90, 97, 98 and 104.

Origin: Peter Abbott, 1979.

Description: There are no ecclesiastical connections to this walk, it is simply named after the originator. The route is a sample of several other long distance routes including highlights of the Dales Way, the Three Peaks Walk, the Pennine Way and Pennine Link within the Yorkshire Dales and stretches of the Roman Way and Coast to Coast within the Lake District. Badges and certificates are not issued.

Reference: *Abbott's Hike,* P. Abbott. Published by the author in conjunction with Embossograph Printers Ltd, 486 Blackburn Road, Bolton.

The R.E.D. Route

Start – Dacre Banks Youth Hostel, Grid reference 198 618 (optional).
Finish – Ellingstring Youth Hostel, Grid reference 176 835 (optional).
Distance – 25 miles (40 km).
Map – O.S. Sheet 99 (1:50,000).

Origin: Youth Hostels Association, Yorkshire Region, 1981.

Description: A route through Upper Nidderdale connecting the hostels at Ramsgill, Ellingstring and Dacre Banks. Open to YHA members only (see page   for details).

Further Information: Send a stamped addressed envelope to Mr S. Townson, 18 Victoria Street, Wetherby, West Yorkshire, LS22 4RE.

A Coast to Coast Walk

PILLAR OF STONES – Coldbergh Edge

**Start – St. Bees Head, Cumbria. Finish – Robin Hood's Bay N.Y.
Distance – 190 miles (306 km).   Ascent – 16,000 feet (4,876 m).
Maps – O.S. Sheets 89, 90, 91, 93, 94, 98, 99 (1:50,000).
          O.S. Tourist Maps, Lake District and North York Moors.
Links – Yorkshire Dales: Pennine Way, Yoredale Way, Yorkshire
          Dales Centurion Walk, Eden Way.
          Lake District: Pennine Link, Roman Way, Cumbria Way.
          North York Moors: Cleveland Way.**

Introduction: An impressive and inspiring journey from the Irish
Sea to the North Sea devised by Alfred Wainwright and published
in 1972 to encourage walkers to take out the map and pioneer their
own routes, rather than following in the footsteps of officialdom. In
the style of his Lakeland guidebooks and *Pennine Way Companion*
he has set a classic example. The 190 mile route links the St. Bees
Head, south of Whitehaven, with Robin Hood's Bay, near Whitby;
passes through the Lake District, Yorkshire Dales and North York
Moors National Parks; uses rights of way throughout and goes over
high ground where possible. Certainly one of the finest walks in
England which should rank high on the list of any experienced long
distance walker.

The Yorkshire Dales section of the path takes in some wild and beautiful country. From Kirkby Stephen it crosses the Pennine Watershed at Nine Standards Rigg, follows the Whitsundale Valley to Keld then climbs to the high moors above Swaledale to explore some interesting and long abandoned mines before arriving at Reeth. From here a delightful stretch near the Swale takes the walker to historic Richmond, dominated by its majestic Norman keep.

Completions: Completions are not recorded; certificates and badges are not issued. Although there are no official recordings the fastest known crossing is by P. Simpson and F. Thomas in 2 days 3 hours 10 minutes.

Reference: *A Coast to Coast Walk,* Alfred Wainwright (Westmorland Gazette, 1972).

ROUTE OUTLINE						ROUTE LOG	
NO	GRID REF	LOCATION	HEIGHT feet	DISTANCE mls	km	DATE	TIME
1	960 118	ST BEES	50	0	0		
2	069 159	ENNERDALE	400	14	22		
3	259 148	ROSTHWAITE	500	29	46		
4	398 159	PATTERDALE	600	47	75		
5	562 154	SHAP	900	63	101		
6	774 087	KIRKBY STEPHEN	600	83	133		
7	892 011	KELD	1100	95	153		
8	038 993	REETH	700	107	172		
9	171 009	RICHMOND	400	117	188		
10	337 986	DANBY WISKE	200	131	210		
11	449 007	INGLEBY CROSS	200	140	224		
12	573 033	CLAY BANK	850	152	243		
13	679 997	BLAKEY	1300	161	258		
14	783 056	GLAISDALE	300	171	274		
15	892 024	MAY BECK	500	180	288		
16	953 049	ROBIN HOOD'S BAY	50	190	304		

COAST TO COAST WALK

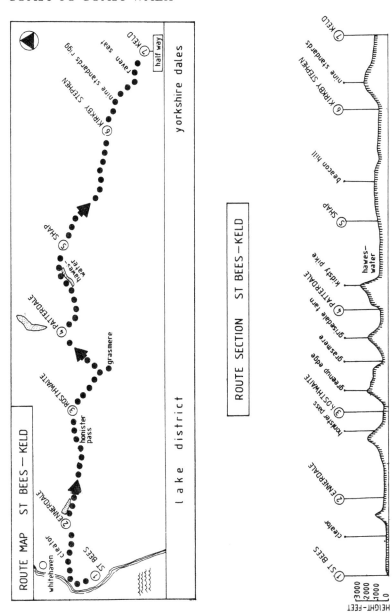

ROUTE MAP   ST BEES — KELD

lake district

yorkshire dales

ROUTE SECTION   ST BEES — KELD

whitehaven
cleator
ST BEES (1)
(2) ENNERDALE
honister pass
(3) ROSTHWAITE
grasmere
(4) PATTERDALE
hawes-water
(5) SHAP
nine standards rigg
(6) KIRKBY STEPHEN
raven seat
(7) KELD
half way

ST BEES (1)
cleator
(2) ENNERDALE
honister pass
(3) ROSTHWAITE
greenup edge
grasmere
grisedale tarn
(4) PATTERDALE
kidsty pike
hawes-water
(5) SHAP
beacon hill
nine standards
(6) KIRKBY STEPHEN
(7) KELD

HEIGHT—FEET
3000
2000
1000
0
miles

48

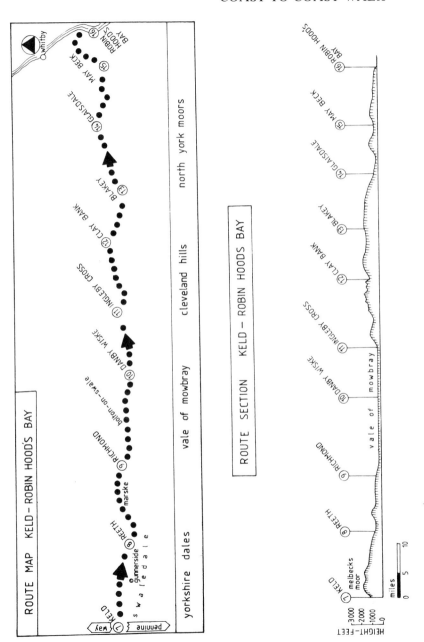

ROUTE MAP KELD–ROBIN HOOD'S BAY

pennine way — ① KELD — swaledale — gunnerside — ⑧ REETH — marske — ⑨ RICHMOND — bolton-on-swale — ⑩ DANBY W/SKE — ⑪ INGLEBY CROSS — ⑫ CLAY BANK — ⑬ BLAKEY — ⑭ GLAISDALE — ⑮ MAY BECK — ⑯ ROBIN HOODS BAY — Whitby

yorkshire dales | vale of mowbray | cleveland hills | north york moors

ROUTE SECTION KELD – ROBIN HOODS BAY

① KELD / melbecks moor — ⑧ REETH — ⑨ RICHMOND — vale of mowbray — ⑩ DANBY W/SKE — ⑪ INGLEBY CROSS — ⑫ CLAY BANK — ⑬ BLAKEY — ⑭ GLAISDALE — ⑮ MAY BECK — ⑯ ROBIN HOODS BAY

HEIGHT–FEET
3000
2000
1000
0

miles
0 5 10

The Dales Way

There must be dales in Paradise
Else what will dalesman do
Throughout the long eternities,
And none to wander through!
Where walk and sing and laugh and laike
Before the rest of heaven's awake?

from 'Dales in Paradise'
A. J. Brown, 1948

Start – Ilkley Bridge.   **Finish – Bowness-on-Windermere.**
Distance – 81 miles (130 km).   **Ascent – 3,200 feet (975 m).**
Maps – O.S. Sheets 97, 98, 104 (1:50,000).
     Outdoor Leisure Maps (1:25,000) Malham and Upper
     Wharfedale, Three Peaks, English Lakes South-East.
Links – Ebor Way, Pennine Way, Yoredale Way, Pennine Link.

Introduction: A pleasant riverside walk from the edge of industrial West Yorkshire to South Lakeland through the heart of the Dales. Conceived by Tom Wilcock, the walk was inaugurated by the West Riding Ramblers' Association in 1968. It was the first of many unofficial long distance routes which now traverse our northern hills. Gentle walking predominates with the maximum height of 1,700 feet being reached at Cam Head where it crosses the Pennine Way. From this point navigation becomes increasingly less obvious and careful use of the 1:25,000 maps, where available, is strongly recommended. Fascinating links from Leeds, Bradford and Harrogate make it possible for the city dweller to literally step out of his door and walk to the shores of Windermere in the Lake District.

Completions: Completions are not recorded; badges and certificates are not isued.

References:
The Dales Way, Colin Speakman (Dalesman Books, 1970).
Dales Way Companion, West Riding Ramblers' Association. Contains accommodation and public transport information. Send a stamped addressed envelope for details to Ramblers' Association, 1/5 Wandsworth Road, London, SW8 2LJ.
Parklink Walks in Upper Wharfedale, Arthur Gemmell (Stile Publications, 1978), Mercury House, Morley, West Yorkshire, LS21 3HE.

Note: Two barns at Cam Houses and Cat Holes (Sedbergh) have been converted by the National Park Authority to provide basic but

ROUTE OUTLINE					
NO	GRID REF	LOCATION	HEIGHT feet	DISTANCE mls	km
1	113 482	ILKLEY BRIDGE	78	0	0
2	071 523	BOLTON ABBEY	114	6	10
3	999 639	GRASSINGTON	550	19	30
4	940 773	BUCKDEN	750	31	50
5	824 821	CAM HOUSES FARM	1450	41	66
6	707 872	DENT BRIDGE	450	52	84
7	661 913	MILLTHROP BRIDGE	350	58	93
8	568 966	GRAYRIGG FOOT	400	69	111
9	470 978	STAVELEY	350	76	122
10	402 961	BOWNESS	100	81	130

ROUTE LOG	
DATE	TIME

ROUTE SECTION

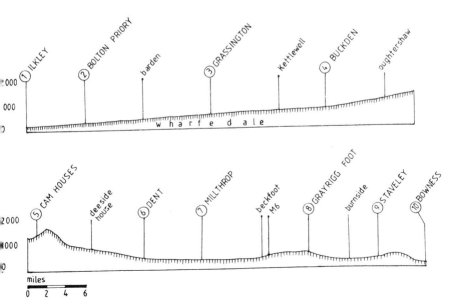

51

DALES WAY

THE DALES WAY CAIRN

popular overnight accommodation. Enquiries to National Park Office, Hebden Road, Grassington, Skipton, North Yorkshire.

The Dales Way Links

Leeds Dales Way Link

Start – Hyde Park Corner, Woodhouse Moor, Leeds (Grid reference 297 355).
Finsih – Ilkley Bridge (Grid reference 113 482).
Distance – 20 miles (32 km).
Map – O.S. Sheet 104.

Origin: Leeds Ramblers' Association, 1973.

Description: A route from the heart of Leeds via the Meanwood Valley, Adel Beck, Eccup Reservoir, Bramhope, Otley Chevin, Burley Woodhead and Ilkley Moor to join the Dales Way at Ilkley Bridge.

Further Information: *Footpaths of Leeds – A Guide* (Leeds Ramblers' Association Footpath Group and the Leeds Civic Trust, 1973) describes the Leeds to Bramhope section.

Harrogate Dales Way Link

Start – Valley Gardens, Harrogate (Grid reference 297 553)
Finish – Cavendish Pavilion, Bolton Abbey (Grid reference 077 552).
Distance – 20 miles (32 km).
Map – 0.S. Sheet 104.

Origin: Harrogate Ramblers' Association, opened in 1974.

Description: A link to the Dales Way via Havarah Park, the Washburn Valley and Rocking Hall Moor.

Further Information: A route description of the walk is to be included in the booklet *Further Walks around Harrogate* to be published in 1982. Enquiries with stamped addressed envelope to P. L. Goldsmith, 20 Pannal Ash Grove, Harrogate, HG2 0HZ.

Bradford Dales Way Link

No information has been published on this so why not take out the map and devise your own route!

The Towpath Trod

Start – Leeds (Grid reference 303 331).
Finish – Skipton (Grid reference 986 516).
Distance – 29 miles (46km).
Maps – O.S. Sheets 103, 104 (1:50,000).

Origin: West Riding Ramblers' Association, 1969.

Description: *The Towpath Trod* was the name of a booklet (not currently available) produced jointly by the West Riding Area of the Ramblers' Association and the North Eastern Branch of the Inland Waterways Association in 1969. Although not rights of way, canal towpaths offer further possibilities to enhance the scope of long distance walking and the Countryside Commission is currently investigating their full recreational potential. As already demonstrated by *The Towpath Trod* it is not necessary to wait for any official blessings to take a stroll along the historic Leeds and Liverpool canal. The minor eyesores are more than made up for by the long stretches of unspoilt countryside and variety of architectural and engineering features.

Further Information: Send stamped addressed envelope with enquiries regarding the future availability of *The Towpath Trod* to E. M. Green, 5 Huby Banks, Huby, Leeds, LS17 0AN.

The Yoredale Way

Start – York.
Finish – Kirkby Stephen.
Distance – 100 miles (160 km).
Ascent – 5,500 feet (1,676 m).
Maps – O.S. Sheets 91, 98, 99, 105, (1:50,000).
Links – Pennine Way, Coast to Coast, Yorkshire Centurion, Eden Way.

Introduction: A 100 mile route between York and Kirkby Stephen which follows the course of the River Ure (anciently known as the Yore) from the point at which it joins the River Ouse 10 miles north of York to Ure Head, 2,000 feet above sea level among the Pennine fells between Hawes and Kirkby Stephen. First completed by Ken Piggin, noted for pioneering the Ebor Way, this is a route designed for walkers who like to take their time and explore the countryside.

The walk traverses the York plain taking in the Devil's Arrows near Boroughbridge, Ripon, the picturesque village of West Tanfield, Jervaulx Abbey and Middleham Castle before reaching Leyburn on the edge of the Dales. An excursion to the summit of Pen Hill provides excellent views along Wensleydale before continuing to West Burton and onto the famous waterfalls at Aysgarth and Hardraw. The final section includes Cotterdale, Hell Gill gorge and Ure Head followed by a pleasant walk alongside the river Eden visiting Pendragon and Lammerside Castles. An attractive, leisurely route with pleasant villages and market towns providing welcome refreshment stops. The walk may be completed in either direction, as a continuous exercise or in random sections to suit your convenience.

Completions: Badges and certificates are available for successful completions. Send a stamped addressed envelope for details to K. E. Piggin, 95 Bishopthorpe Road, York, YO2 1NX (no personal callers please).

Reference: *The Yoredale Way,* J. K. E. Piggin (Dalesman Books, 1980)

YOREDALE WAY

ROUTE OUTLINE					
NO	GRID REF	LOCATION	HEIGHT feet	\<br\>mls	DISTANCE\<br\>km
1	600 521	YORK MUSEUM GDNS	35	O	O
2	511 599	NEWTON ON OUSE	50	9	14
3	396 669	BOROUGHBRIDGE	50	20	32
4	315 712	RIPON	100	28	45
5	225 810	MASHAM	250	40	64
6	114 904	LEYBURN	650	54	86
7	O11 886	AYSGARTH	588	68½	110
8	873 898	HAWES	800	79	126
9	796 948	GARSDALE HEAD	1250	87	139
10	774 083	KIRKBY STEPHEN	600	100	160

ROUTE LOG	
DATE	TIME

ROUTE SECTION

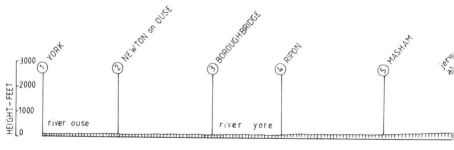

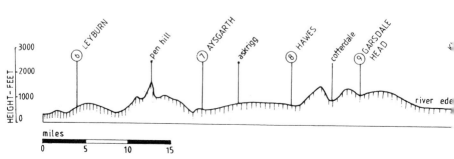

56

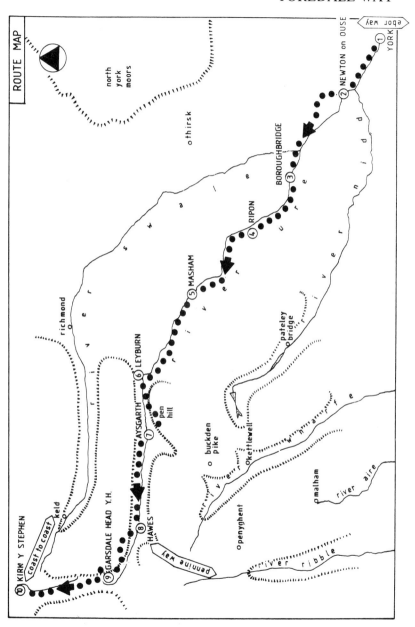

ROUTE MAP

The Yorkshire Dales Centurion Walk

Start and finish – Horton-in-Ribblesdale.
Distance – 100 miles (160 km).
Ascent – 16,000 feet (4,876m).
Maps — o.s. Sheets 91, 92, 97, 98,
(1:50,000).
Links – Dales Way, Yoredale Way,
Pennine Way, Coast to Coast, Eden Way,

Introduction: This outstanding walk, encompassing the major dales and outer fells of the Yorkshire Dales National Park, was conceived by Jonathan Ginesi whose guide was first published in 1976. Yorkshire's best known peaks, wild moorland, the fine walking country of the Howgills and a visit to England's highest inn at Tan Hill, 1,732 feet, all make for a challenging and rewarding journey that should not be missed.

Completions: Badges are available for successful completions from Mr P. Bayes, Pen-y-Ghent Stores, Horton-in-Ribblesdale, Settle, North Yorkshire, BD24 0HE.

Reference:
Official Guide Book to the Yorkshire Dales Centurion Walk, Jonathan Ginesi (John Siddall (Printers) Limited, 1976).
Adventure plan, Jonathan Ginesi (John Sidall (Printers) Ltd, 1981).

ROUTE OUTLINE						ROUTE LOG	
NO	GRID REF	LOCATION	HEIGHT feet	DISTANCE mls	km	DATE	TIME
1	807 725	HORTON	790	0	0		
2	742 746	INGLEBOROUGH	2373	5	8		
3	743 776	CHAPEL LE DALE	975	8	13		
4	738 814	WHERNSIDE	2419	10½	17		
5	705 870	DENT	460	16½	26		
6	657 922	SEDBERGH	475	21½	34		
7	667 971	THE CALF	2219	25½	41		
8	724 040	RAVENSTONEDALE	800	32½	52		
9	775 086	KIRKBY STEPHEN	550	38	61		
10	825 061	NINE STANDARDS RIGG	2171	42½	68		
11	897 067	TAN HILL INN	1732	47½	76		
12	946 043	LEVEL	1750	51½	82		

YORKSHIRE DALES CENTURION WALK

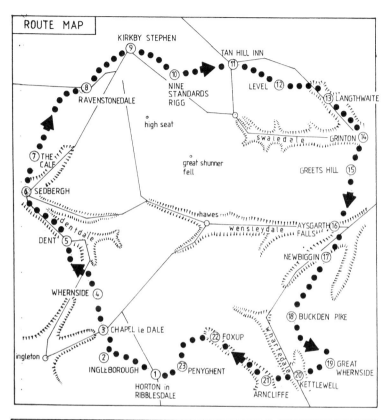

ROUTE ROUTE					
NO	GRID REF	LOCATION	HEIGHT feet	DISTANCE mls	km
13	005 025	LANGTHWAITE	850	56½	90
14	046 984	GRINTON	600	61	98
15	028 957	GREETS HILL	1676	63½	102
16	011 886	AYSGARTH FALLS	588	69½	111
17	001 857	NEWBIGGIN	650	72½	116
18	961 788	BUCKDEN PIKE	2302	78	125
19	002 739	GREAT WHERNSIDE	2310	82½	132
20	972 723	KETTLEWELL	700	85	136
21	933 719	ARNCLIFFE	740	87½	140
22	872 767	FOXUP	1020	93	149
23	838 734	PEN-Y-GHENT	2273	97½	156
24	807 725	HORTON	790	100	160

ROUTE LOG	
DATE	TIME

YORKSHIRE DALES CENTURION WALK

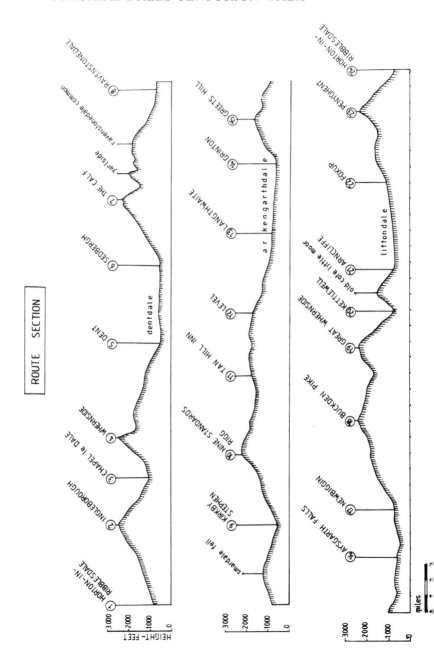

ROUTE SECTION

A Coast to Coast II

Start – Arnside, Cumbria (Grid reference 457 788).
Finish – Saltburn-by-the-Sea, Cleveland (Grid reference 665 215).
Distance – 120 miles (193 km).
Maps – O.S. Sheets 93, 97, 98, 99.

Origin: R. French, 1979.

Description: Another example of the variety of routes which can be devised between the west and east coasts. The route takes a more southerly approach than Wainwright's, going from Morecambe Bay to Kirkby Lonsdale and Ribblehead, then through Wensleydale to Leyburn. From here it crosses the Vale of York to Osmotherley where it joins the Cleveland Way which is followed to Saltburn-by-the-Sea.

Further Information: For details of *A One Week Coast to Coast Walk,* printed sheets containing a brief outling of the route and accommodation, send a stamped addressed envelope to the following address: R. French, National Park Warden, Wilkin Stile, Dowbiggin, Sedbergh, Cumbria.

Harrogate Inner Ring (Proposed)

Start and finish – Knaresborough, North Yorkshire (Grid reference 345 571).
Distance – 20 miles (32km).
Map – O.S. Sheets 104 (1:50,000).

Origin: Elizabeth M. Carroll, 1978, Harrogate Ramblers' Association.

Description: A short radius circuit of the town using footpaths through the Crimple Valley, Oakdale and the Nidd Valley. The walk can be walked in three easy stages using public transport.

Further Information: A full route description will be included in *Further Walks around Harrogate* due for publication in 1982. Send a stamped addressed envelope with enquiries to P. L Goldsmith, 20 Pannal Ash Grove, Harrogate, North Yorkshire, HG2 0HZ.

Connecting Routes from Adjacent Areas

Pennine Link	**70 miles (113 km)**
Eden Way	**68 miles (109 km)**
Ebor way	**70 miles (113 km)**

Ebor Way – North York Moors

A 70 mile walk from Helmsley, the start of the Cleveland Way, to Ilkley, the start of the Dales Way, passing through York where it also links with the Yoredale Way.

Reference:
The Ebor Way, J. K. E. Piggin (Dalesman Books, 1978).
Long Distance Walks, Volume One – North York Moors and Wolds, T. Wimbush (Dalesman Books, 1981).

Pennine Link – Lake District

The Pennine Link connects the Pennine Way at Horton-in-Ribblesdale to Keswick in the Lake District in a 70 mile route passing through Ribblehead and Dentdale.

Reference: *Across Northern Hills*, G. Berry (Westmorland Gazette, 1975).

Eden Way – North Pennines

A 68 mile route following the river Eden from its source in the Yorkshire Dales Mallerstang area to Wetheral near Carlisle.

Reference: *Across Northern Hills*, G. Berry (Westmorland Gazette, 1955).

General Notes

Safety on Open Challenge Walks

1. A sound knowledge and experience of map reading, equipment and safety are necessary under conditions which can induce fatigue and impair judgement.

2. Devise a route schedule taking into account the hours of daylight available and check your progess against it.

3. In order to eliminate the risk of navigational errors, if possible survey the route beforehand in sections, making notes and taking any compass bearings that may be required.

4. If you have a support party ensure everyone knows precisely when and where you are to rendezvous. Failure of support parties to locate walkers can lead to rescue teams being needlessly called out. Arrange a central telephone point so that messages can be passed on if you decide to retire or inform the police so that time is not wasted looking for you.

5. Leave word of your route and make sure there are at least three people in your party.

6. Obtain a local weather forecast before setting out and be prepared for the worst; sudden weather changes are common.

7. Note the location of telephone boxes and possible escape routes.

8. The distress signal is six blows of a whistle or six flashes of a torch at one minute intervals.

Sponsored Walks

Sponsored walks in the countryside involving distances over 20 miles have become a popular means of fund raising. As such walks often involve individuals not accustomed to walking long distances it is essential that all aspects of organisation and safety are fully considered. To this end and Ramblers' Association has published a booklet entitled *Sponsored Walks in the Countryside*. For details send a stamped addressed envelope to the Ramblers' Association, 1/5 Wandsworth Road, London, SW8 2LJ.

Equipment for Challenge Walks

1. Checklist for open Challenge Walks
- Map and map case.
- Compass.
- Whistle.
- Walk schedule and pencil.
- Spare jumper.
- Food to eat en-route.
- Drink.
- Torch, spare batteries and bulb.
- Spare socks.
- Waterproof jacket and overtrousers.
- Polythene survival bag.
- Two fivepence pieces for telephone calls.
- Emergency rations.
- Woollen hat.
- Boots with patterned sole and ankle support.
- First aid kit.

2. The rules of challenge events specify precisely what equipment is to be worn or carried. These should be strictly adhered to otherwise disqualification will result. In addition to the items listed above events are likely to specify the following:
- Exact contents of First aid kit.
- Mug.

3. This book has been written for experienced walkers. A sound knowledge and experience of equipment and clothing needs has been assumed. Beyond meeting basic requirements equipment is very much a matter of individual preference. It is emphasised that equipment does not necessarily have to be costly; fashionable, expensive gear does not make a good walker!

4. Prospective long distance walkers should pay particular attention to footwear. Generally as long as boots provide ankle support and have a deep patterned sole then the lighter the better. Heavy boots with rigid soles and stiff uppers will probably be more expensive, take a lot of breaking-in and rapidly sap energy. Light flexible boots are likely to prove less expensive and least troublesome for long distance walking. They can be obtained with a deep ripple or studded sole which provides a grip comparable with the traditional vibram sole. Below is a list of suppliers which specialise in lightweight boots; write for details:
Pete Bland Sports, 12 Danes Road, Staveley, Kendal, Cumbria.
J. A. Jones (Mining), P.O.Box 8, Glossop, Derbyshire, SK13 9UP.

Guide lines on eating and drinking during Challenge Walks

1.   There are no miracle foods or drinks which make the Three Peaks feel like an afternoon stroll! Food taken en-route has a limited influence over performance. The long-term effects of bodily adjustment to long distance walking combined with inherent ability are much more important factors.

2.   A general rule for eating during demanding walks is little and often so that the body does not become overloaded with the burden of digestion as well as muscular activity.

3.   Generally, your body is the best guide to immediate food and drink requirements. As muscle activity and sweat loss deplete the body of vital substances, preferences for types of food change. Foods which are readily attractive, palatable and digestable under normal conditions can differ from those required after 30 miles and fatigue has set in. Discovering which foods do or do not suit you is largely a matter of trial and error.

4.   During hot weather when sweat loss is great, drinking at frequent intervals is important, especially for runners, otherwise dehydration may result. This is a remote prospect in this country but the consequences can be serious including permanent disablement and death.

5.   It is common knowledge that sweating is not just a matter of water loss. Salt tablets (sodium chloride) are often taken during hot weather to avoid cramp. However, potassium and magnesium losses are just as important as sodium. Specialist drinks are available which help replace the body salts lost in activity. Staminade is a brand popular among some long distance walkers as it is available as a powder which can be mixed with water at convenient stopping points. It also contains glucose to aid energy output. Write for local stockists to Nicholas Laboratories Limited, Slough, SL1 4AU.

6.   Sweet foods are usually consumed to assist energy output. Glucose is the fastest acting source of energy. In liquid form it will cause a rise in blood sugar in approximately half an hour. The rule of little and often applies, particularly to glucose and other forms of sugar such as chocolate, otherwise the body will over-react producing a low blood sugar level which will ultimately leave you feeling more fatigued.

7.   A common myth among active people is the need for plenty of protein. Several experiments have shown protein loss during activity to be no greater that when at rest. Eating protein foods will do nothing to aid performance; indeed, many modern nutritionists consider high protein intake, especially meat, to be damaging to health.

8. Listed below are some of the most popular foods consumed during demanding walks:

- Rice pudding and tinned fruit.
- Jam sandwiches.
- Salad sandwiches.
- Cake (all varieties).
- Chocolate (all varieties).
- Fresh fruit.
- Sweet tea.
- Staminade.
- Complan food drink.
- Glucose tablets (maximum of two each hour).

Reference: *Food for Fitness* (World Publications, U.S.A., 1975). Available from Running Wild, 2 Tower Street, Hyde, Cheshire.

The Countryside Commision

1. The Countryside Commission was brought into being under the 1968 Countryside Act when it assumed the functions of the National Parks Commission set up in 1949. Its powers were then enhanced by the 1974 Local Government Act. Matters relating to long distance footpaths and bridleways, National Parks, Areas of Outstanding Natural Beauty, Heritage Coasts, country parks, picnic sites, research and publicity all come within the control of the Countryside Commission.

2. The following publicity leaflets are currently available from the Countryside Commission, John Dower House, Crescent Place, Cheltenham, Glouscestershire, GL40 3RA. Telephone Cheltenham 21381.

- *Long Distance Footpaths and Bridleways* – an illustrated leaflet on all the twelve paths currently approved.
- *Recreational Paths* – a county by county summary of some of the long distance routes which have been sponsored by County Councils, voluntary organisations and individuals.
- *The Countryside Commission* – a brief explanation of its functions.
- *National Parks of England and Wales* – an illustrated leaflet describing all ten National Parks.
- *The Pennine Way* – an illustrated leaflet of the route.
- *Yorkshire Dales National Park* – an illustrated leaflet.
- *Public Transport in the National Parks* – a summary of public transport facilities.

The Yorkshire Dales National Park

1. The Yorkshire Dales was designated as a National Park in 1954 following the principles laid down in the National Parks and Access to Countryside Act of 1949. It is administered by the Yorkshire Dales National Park Committee which has a duty of both protecting the exceptional beauty of the landscape and promoting its enjoyment by the public. To help achieve these objectives information centres have been set up to provide a comprehensive service to visitors. The National Park Centres are listed below:

- Aysgarth Falls — Telephone Aysgarth 424.
- Clapham — Telephone Clapham 419.
- Grassington — Telephone Grassington 752748.
- Hawes — Telephone Hawes 450.
- Malham — Telephone Airton 363.
- Sedbergh — Telephone Sedbergh 20125.

2. An extensive range of books and leaflets is available from the National Park office which includes general information and accommodation. A leaflet entitled *Stay in a Dales Barn* is of particular interest to Dales Way and Pennine Way walkers. For a complete list of publications write to the National Park Office, 'Colvend', Hebden Road, Grassington, Skipton, North Yorkshire, BD23 5LB.

3. Comprehensive information on accommodation, including camping, is also published by the Yorkshire Dales Tourist Association, Burnsall, Skipton, North Yorkshire, BD23 6BP. Telephone 075-672 668.

Public Transport in the National Park

Dales Rail

A special rail charter service, with connecting buses, which operates on certain weekends between April and October from Leeds, Bradford, Keighley Skipton, Preston, Blackburn and Carlisle. Details obtainable from West Yorkshire Passenger Transport Executive, Metro House, West Parade, Wakefield, West Yorkshire, WF1 1NS. Telephone Wakefield 78234.

Parklink

A combined rail and bus ticket serving Wharfedale, Malhamdale or Ribblesdale to encourage the use of public transport in the Dales. The Parklink leaflet is available from British Rail stations in West

Yorkshire or from National Park Centres (see above).
Parklink Walks in Upper Wharfedale, Arthur Gemmell (Stile Publications, 1978) Mercury House, Otley, West Yorkshire, LS21 3HE.

Scheduled Rail Services

For information on the following lines contact your local railway station.
* Leeds — Skipton — Morecambe
* Leeds and Bradford — Ilkley
* Leeds — Settle — Carlisle

Dales Rider

A bus ticket providing ulimited travel on West Yorkshire Road Car Transport Company services in the Dales area. See below for timetable details.

Scheduled Bus Services

Full details of all bus services in the Yorkshire Dales can be obtained in timetables from the following operators shown below. Send a stamped addressed envelope for prices of timetables.
* West Yorkshire Road Car Company Limited, East Parade, Harrogate, North Yorkshire – telephone Harrogate 66061.
* United Automobile Service Limited, United House, Grange Road, Darlington, Co. Durham, DL1 5NL – telephone Darlington 652552.
* Ribble Motor Services Limited, Frenchwood Avenue, Preston, Lancashire, PR1 4LU – telephone Preston 54754.
* Pennine Motor Services Limited, West Street, Gargrave, Skipton, North Yorkshire – telephone Gargrave 215.

Publications

Send a stamped addressed envelope for details of the following information to the National Park Office, 'Colvend', Hebden Road, Grassington, Skipton, North Yorkshire, BD23 5LB.
* *Transport Information Pack.*
* *Getting around the Yorkshire Dales.*

Organisations

Long Distance Walkers' Association

The L.D.W.A. was founded in 1972 by Alan Blatchford and Chris Steer. Although it encompasses all categories of long distance walking, it caters primarily for those interested in challenge walks. There is now a dedicated following of some three thousand members with local groups in most parts of the country including North Yorkshire, West Yorkshire and Teesside. Since it was founded the L.D.W.A. has lived up to its name by promoting a series of hundred mile challenge events starting in 1973 with the Downsman Hundred. There then followed the Peakland Hundred in 1974, a second Downsman in 1975, the Cleveland Hundred in 1976, a third Downsman in 1977, a second Cleveland in 1978, a Dartmoor Hundred in 1979, a fourth Downsman in 1980 and finally a Cumbrian Hundred (optional 200 kilometres) in 1981.

One of the main attractions of membership is the newsletter appropriately called *Strider*. Edited by Chris Steer it is packed with news of the local group activities, a comprehensive calendar of challenge events, reports on past events, general articles plus news and views from the members.

For membership details send a stamped addressed envelope to the following address:
L.D.W.A. Membership Secretary, 4 Mayfield Road, Tunbridge Wells, Kent, TN4 8ES.

The Ramblers' Association

Every walker in the countryside is indebted to the Ramblers' Association. It helps to preserve the footpath network by opposing unwarranted diversions and closures; conserves our natural heritage against encroachment; opposes harmful legislation and helps promote recreational walking and the appreciation of the countryside. The Ramblers' Association has played an important role in the creation of both official long distance paths and recreational paths.

Membership includes the receipt of a comprehensive bed and breakfast guide, receipt of their magazine *Rucksack* and local walk programmes. For membership and details send a large stamped addressed envelope to the following address;
The Ramblers' Association, 1/5 Wandsworth Road, London, SW8 2LJ.

The British Orienteering Federation

Write for details to British Orienteering Federation, National Office, Lea Green, Near Matlock, Derbyshire, DE4 5GJ.

The Fell Runners' Association

The F.R.A. exists to encourage and foster better standards of fell running and allied mountain racing throughout the United Kingdom. Membership includes the receipt of *The Fell Runner* magazine and a fell running calendar of events. For membership details send stamped addressed envelope to the following address: N. F. Berry, 165 Penistone Road, Kirkburton, Huddersfield, HD8 0PH.

The Youth Hostels Association

The Y.H.A. was founded to help all, especially young people of limited means, to a greater knowledge and care of the countryside. This is done by providing hostels or other simple accommodation throughout the country. Write for membership details to Y.H.A., National Office, St Albans, Hertfordshire, AL1 2DY.

The Madhatters

This is the name of a club proposed by Peter Travis in 1979 which involves itself in undertaking strenuous activities such as long distance walking in order to help worthy causes. The activities undertaken should reflect the club's motto 'Achieve and Serve' by both making exceptional demands on the ability of the member and raising money to benefit the less fortunate. Send a stamped addressed envelope for details to Peter Travis, 23 Kingsway East, Westlands, Newcastle, Staffordshire, ST5 3PY.

Commons, Open Spaces and Footpaths Preservation Society

Founded in 1865, the Society aims to promote knowledge of the law so that paths and commons may be preserved for the public benefit. Send a stamped addressed envelope for details of membership to the following address: 25A Bell Street, Henley-on-Thames, Oxon, RG9 2BA.

Walk Logs

DATE	OPEN CHALLENGE WALK	DISTANCE	TOTAL TIME

WALK LOGS

DATE	CHALLENGE EVENT	DISTANCE	TOTAL TIME	POSITION	STARTERS / FINISHERS

LONG DISTANCE FOOTPATHS AND RECREATIONAL PATHS	DISTANCE	START DATE	FINISH DATE	TOTAL TIME